16   1.99

CONGREVE'S BALSAMIC ELIXIR

GW00384164

Congreve's Balsamic Elixir

FREDERICK JONES

PETERLOO POETS

First published in 1995
by Peterloo Poets
2 Kelly Gardens, Calstock, Cornwall PL18 9SA, U.K.

© 1995 by Frederick Jones

All rights reserved. No part of this publication may be
reproduced, stored in a retrieval system, or transmitted,
in any form or by any means, electronic, mechanical,
photocopying, recording or otherwise without the prior
permission in writing of the publisher.

A catalogue record for this book is available
from the British Library

ISBN 1-871471-49-4

Printed in Great Britain by
Latimer Trend & Company Ltd, Plymouth

ACKNOWLEDGEMENTS: Some of these poems have appeared in the following magazines: *Envoi, Orbis, Outposts, Pennine Platform, Poetry and Audience, Poetry Nottingham, Recorder, Scratch, Smith's Knoll, Staple, Verse, Weyfarers.*

Five appeared (as a winning entry in the 1991 Northern Poetry Competition) in *Northern Poetry Two* (Littlewood, 1991).

Twelve appeared in *Peterloo Preview 3* (1993).

'Cairns' was awarded the Felicia Hemans Prize for Lyrical Poetry for 1992.

The tide of mere plurality
Breaks upon the esplanade.

Contents

Adventure

Today it's autumn (spring). The washed out sun
is streaky, a fresh air slaps across the street,
restless, volatile, buoyant. Anything
could happen today (could have happened).

At the bus stop a face
seems to impart the secrets of the soul —
somehow it won't go into words.
The form of this is '(A entails B) and (A and not B)'.

Logic is tautology. All of a sudden,
the temperature drops a million degrees
like a childhood Christmas or better still
the week before Christmas, and the soul

becomes a vast expanse of milky
light. If there is an afterlife
I think that this is what it's like.

Four Seasons

1.
A woodbird sings
in the heart of oak;
a crisp sunny wind.

2.
Suddenly the light
moves out of focus, an
intuition trickling away
irreparably.

3.
Light swirls in the street.
It is a child's toy, a town
in a jar: shake it
and there will be snow,
the brandy's heartbeat in the throat.

4.
An icy splinter of sun
pierces to the bones of the morning,
windpicked till there's
nothing left but spirit.

Congreve's Balsamic Elixir

Trapped in a warren of thoughts that hound
my steps I crawl along the pit of lime
to the Sunday Market and wander round
the ragbag of stalls. After a long time

I could still be doing the same,
sifting jumble, wondering if feeling's
returned. A will o' the wisp of calm
flits somewhere between the peeling

enamelware, the rusty biscuit
tins, pock-marked mangles and wonky globes,
jetsam whose intimations of lost hopes

and endless wear are like a vaccine.
Caught by some old bottles' milky green
I pick up one to feel, and hold it.

Undoing the Thread

This was in my dreams: a cottage,
a comb of pines leading tractors and cows
to the big house, the knotted oak. Beyond that
stubble corn and sea haze, and the sun

ripening the shadows on the hills. The surface
has broken. People good and bad as always,
but calloused against the earth. A year
evicted by a farmer's wife, who gave

without kindness, received without enjoyment:
looking back, even the past is changing
as the road winds in and out
of the rain, the grey light.

Orkney Tombstones

No manners at all, has Death,
won't hang on for a minute
while you just nip to the toilet,
just puts the boot in in front of your friends
or at the theatre, and you lose control
and fill your pants; meanwhile he wastes
a busload, or decimates a continent
with an unphotogenic disease.
His performance has the total
autonomy of great art as he goes on
composing his masterpiece, the epic
Complete Catalogue of the Human Race —
musicians, short order cooks, irritating
younger brothers, the fair haired
and hazel eyed, the old and maimed,
erotic dancers, chartists: everyone
is registered in a niche of their own
like Herodotus' list of the dead
at Thermopylae, or the plaques
and memorials in this distant island
Cathedral, its red stone wormed out
by rain and sea haar, their deaths
in foreign parts gathered and treasured,
missionaries, traders, explorers,
along the walls one Canto will transcribe.

Evening Walk (Iltakävely)

In the evening,
tired of the light I go for a walk
I'm not used to the light
I'm not used to you
     you and the spring,
         prima vera
         prima vista
          & sight for sore eyes:
What happens when time exceeds the speed of light?
   At the junction an angel signals with white gloves

(Annukka Peura, Finnish, b. 1968)

Cairns

It starts as a game. Your son is worn out
from the steep heathscrub where the path frayed
into nothing but the odd cairn choked in ferns,
and cold with the mizzle off the fells, the damp wind.

There'd been the tarn, a grey-green lagoon
of bog-grass and moss hung between clouds and water,
the closeness at the banks, and the sodden slopes
curved round like a theatre to watch some rain

idle across the surface, far from the politics of meaning.
Twenty yards back the drizzle's almost silent
waterclock puts time under the microscope
of its atomic fizz. On the way back,

as the cold and wet sets in, your wife throws
a stone onto a heap by the wayside.
Clack and bounce. It lies in the knobs and gnarls
of pine-root pinning the needle carpet down.

When you pass a cairn you put a stone on.
It's a tradition she tells your son.
And then you're all at it, spying out
the mottled piles perched by spindling rills,

like a game in a children's picture book,
Spot the cairns in the picture. How many
can you find? One stone each clacks and clatters
and goes to keep the track for others who'll make

the journey to the tarn. And in the densest
clag of trees you seed a cairn yourselves, a few
stones each, by the stream below whose froth
you hear a deeper note as black water
tucks air beneath it. *See, now it'll grow.*

St Andrews

Six miles each day I cycle into town,
getting the hang of the road's dips and spirals.
On the map contours give the shape of huge
swirling downs; when you get there, sudden braes
knot the grain of the land. This morning

as I tugged over the high ground the sky
had brightened into rain and I stopped to cool.
The field I'd reached's called Gaston on the map;
two hundred years ago there was a village,
cottages, men with solid, hard-grained lives.

Now nothing of what they were like survives,
the ploughed earth retains no imprint of hearth,
no clumps of crocksherds in the turnip roots;
only the eternal truths cling to the name,
shapeless and vague as ghosts without a home.

Getting it Right

A pile of bricks my children played with
became one sterile afternoon a castle.
For them it's a Crusader Fortress, or
a dungeon denizened with monstrous
monsters, the grimmer the better.
When things get bad, to their delight
I run the curtain wall to a new turret,
begin mining operations, fit jibs
of stick and string to hoist bricksherds up and down —
the image of pointless activity
satisfies, like a rhyme got right.
For me the chains of twisted wire recall
a Piranesi prison, the clanking
of arches and galleries, and stairs winding
like snail tracks through vaulted gloom
where you can catch glimpses of light,
you can even approach them,
but the passage dips or twists, and all
your efforts carry them further away.

Japanese Restaurant

When you're young you think loneliness
is just something that happens to you, say,
if you don't get any letters for a while
or no-one asks you out. It isn't;
it's part of the basic design concept
of the human heart — like Tartini's
Abandoned Dido. Me and the violin.
The girl at the next table wipes
her chopsticks and puts her hair up
with them. My teacher says I should brighten
the tone. 'Don't worry,' she says,
'the dark will still shine through.'

Summer

'Di più direi: ma 'l venire e 'l sermone
più lungo esser non può, pearò ch'i' veggio
là surger nuovo fummo del sabbione.'

*You know that bird that flapped about the beams
during your last exam then disappeared
through an open window — that was my heart
whirring upwards in a sudden access*

*of joy with you the other day. Just once
or twice in a life it's like that; without
the slightest reason you're struck by lightning,
pole-axed, discharging St Elmo's fire from*

every fingertip and you can't tell her
any of it because you're her teacher
and don't belong outside her past, and she

can never even know how special
you thought her, a bird taking wing,
and pulsing in and out of brilliance.

Canto

So much of childhood was grass.
I remember the hours of boredom
at the far end of some field,
the games master's dream of teamship.

The captains believed. They had
so much kudos they didn't know
what to do with it all,
graciously handing it round.

So here I am again, this time
watching my own children
fiddle in the heat hours after
their event. In the end

we avoid the garden party
undetected, the grown-ups playing
at being grown up, and admit
with relief the tedium.

As our train pulls past the school
I watch the silent tumult
swirling after coloured flags,
so many — let's not discuss them.

Summer Walk

Such a hot day, and yet
when I touched a sandstone
wall it was not warm.
Dry and crumbling, spidery
to the fingers. That day
was all bright and overcast,
enough sun for a clear shadow,
but pale under a film of cloud;
and when I sat down
in the park I felt dissolved
in sense, still and excited.
Beneath the surface there is
such a depth of time,
a resonance waiting to be
filled with light.

The Watcher

Next week thrown to the winds
Friends celebrating
Or so I'd guess
With a swim in the sea

A mixed threesome.
Even at this distance
Prurience draws the eye
Can they really be naked?

Imagine
The little heaps of empty clothes hidden
Shapeless in some secluded bay
And them stepping out

Nervous excited
And over the rocks —
How they clamber gingerly
Through daring contortions

Barking shins and toes
On the hardness and sharpness of stone
And down to the waves
To dress in skins of water

Bobbing in and out of the air
And basking on a warm shelf
Until you're in no doubt any more
They're wearing nothing at all

Naked as the Garden of Eden
And rainbow-distant
From the house above the cliff
Where I was a dingy stain on the window

Winter Walk

Walking down to the old part of town
cluttered with white roofs
split by the brown sluggish river,
two roads cut into the mass of buildings
and reveal the shape of the land. That
at least is something. No doubt
each leads somewhere, as if it mattered,
in a maze of cathedral steps,
shop and stall, laced with alleys
worse than a spiral staircase.
A painter leans on the bridge,
distressed by the flow, and waits
for the river to pass him by.
Then he will paint, if a wind
full of snow doesn't alter the glare
just above the top of the road.

Schrödinger's Cat

'Do you remember how we first loved,
that October?' But perhaps she remembers
quite differently, or not at all. Somehow
the truth never quite balances.
I can be anything you want, it breathes,
like some upmarket call-girl.

Horizon

So Tim and that lot took a taxi
and Vicky was sick out of the window —
funny the nostalgia that stirs up.
The twisted rope of pain to unravel

one knot of which is to strain another
further on. I remember it as pure shadow
hanging upright in the deep glare, a black
hole in the bright air. The laws of physics

don't care tuppence for time, but a memory
now, you place it by its warmth and colour,
conker leaves with the light behind them.

Everything must be given up
before the end. Everything.

Oriel

As with a thin rope of stone wall
twisted over mountainside in fog
one knows men have been here before.
Sun and rain and snow, the infinite

gradations of weather have worn
all away here, left only this
window hanging in midair. Standing
in the transient light below, one still

has the sense of a hall. *Where
are they who were before us,
led hounds and bore hawks?
The rich ladies in their bowers*

that wore gold in their tressour? For me
old stones and not glass case items,
illumined patches of a vanished life, tell
that here were people who felt the cold

or opened the window, or realised suddenly
that they had no longer the spirit
or resilience to make such friends
as when they were young.

As I look, sparrows pass in and out
of the embrasure and in a moment's
dropping of the wind I feel a thrill
of recognition recalling Bede:

*This life is like a hall
lit and warmed and full of company
through which a sparrow passes
in the twinkling of an eye
from the dark to the dark again.*

Maze

In those days I worked in the City
traversing the Waste Land endlessly,
endlessly circling the weeks and months,
the dim unspent pages of anger,
dreams unfurled in the dark hours.
At such a distance it seems like
the cold fire of Spring not yet
defeated. Home is where you can never
return, caves buried a thousand years
whose subtext must be prized
out of a dead language and mildewed
frescoes, all that I wormed through
tunnelling out the depths of my
Bluebeard's castle night by night.

Decomposition

Lurking about the house in corners
in cupboards, they whisper quietly
in slow ferment, jars filled
with pickled autumns of dead leaves,

my son's primeval bogs, breeding.
This is the best. Now and then
it moves to the yard, the kitchen window,
or disappears for days or weeks

after a family row. It always comes back,
subtly changed. This that was a leaf —
ages ago its green skins peeled apart,
thinning to a blister of veins traced

in their own clear soup, until
now, only the barest memory
of structure is left,
films wafting in plasma.

Nocturne

Someone else's music
drifts across the night
and in a pool of light

alone the young ones sit
quietly intent on furtive
innocence. Doors shut

and footsteps pass
another way, echoes
in an empty street.

It is different
with older men:
the moonlight brings to mind

Count Dracula in old films,
his infatuated victims,
his alien needs.

The Wind

It could almost have been funny,
so dead on the nail. The dark night
of the soul, the endless anguish,
old snake, lisping its horrible secrets,
true Lear-on-the-heath stuff

blurring without one false note
into a real storm, the worst
recorded gales in England.
Tattered shreds of sleep disperse
to focus on rows of fallen trees,

wrecked cars, houses ripped open.
An outward sign of an inward state.
Tired out and queasy the ghosts
of yesterday flit about
for phone-boxes, picking their way

among rubbish the wind got tired
of breaking. Children are thrilled
at the chaos. Worst of all
the bleak and comfortless sun casts
a naked eye on a few trees

that had stood the nightlong wrenching,
taken the shock and stood —
too weakened to be safe
they're sawn down, ruined things
unfit for their own survival.

Walking in Sibelius Park

The man with a violin beneath his arm
flounders over the crest of a path below a looming sky.
He's not thinking how second rate everything is,
the mender has cured his fiddle, and the blip in his brain
that poked and probed the flaw and squeezed out
every other thought has popped. He's thinking,
The man with a violin beneath his arm
flounders over the crest of a path below a looming sky.
Across the way two young women in jumpers and coats
are pushing their bicycles, pushing their bicycles
and laughing as they swap scale-models of the day's events,
hearts flapping in the wind. This is what it's like
walking in Sibelius Park.

Outcrop

Newcastle, after all this time,
city of girls with lovely voices,
of five bridges; theatres and bars —

thronged with crowds
of the here and now I walk about
light-headed,

absorbed in the lingering
incandescence of late growth,
the flame on the snow;

four years
of parties, books and music;
Turkish cigarettes,

and long games
with language. And love
which took us by surprise.

Long Barrow

A facade of megaliths
like time's ancient choppers
pokes through the hilltop, propping up
a hump of tussocks. Inside,

their bony tenants evicted,
the cool slab chambers almost
suggest a country cottage;
nothing evokes the prehistoric lives.

Nothing but the wads and screws of flowers
and corn dolls that line the walls,
the joss-stick wedged in a crack
by two candles. A gesture

acting itself out, like those
before us we felt stirred
to pick ripe ears of barley
and lay them with the others.

Tenement

I love the backsides of cities,
doggerel districts of dog-eared dogturds
where railway lines intrude on other lives
bare as an electric bulb in rooms

without a curtain. Sandra downstairs,
with her heart-stopping figure, such stuff
as dreams are made of. Someone
had the dream and left the washing up,

the nappies, and the life in a single room.
It's not the mice I mind, creatures of flesh
and fur at least, it's the fat ripe slug
I found this morning, a nasty gob of slime

on the lavatory wall; and how by the time
the kids are in bed we're too tired for sex,
but through the partition I can hear
them screwing for hours next-door.

Ritual

A candle enters, and points of fire spread —
one flame catches even before it's touched
the last; but don't rely on it. Others
are crushed out trying to pass the light on.

The Park

Out of the leaden heat
into this moving light and shade,
an iced drink stills all irritation.
When I look up I see the spilt

ice creams, the harassed mothers
and vacant fathers and one —
two — no, three games of chess,
quietly ticking. Somehow

the scene assumes the green
tranquillity of the aquarium.
In calm clairvoyance the eye
becomes the thing observed.

Wardrobe

Observe the sky in its midmost warmth
the balcony fronting a bright sea
and caught against the light, fumbling
behind the wardrobe door, a girl

in plimsolls, half a bikini,
a blouse unbuttoned — is she dressing
or undressing? this somnolent
perfection is like a work of art,

without before or after;
a lapdog's sinless oblivion.
The glycerine idylls won't lie still;

I have heard since she was raped
at fifteen in a padded cell.

Soda Water

I'm on a bus from Didsbury Village
with a new violinbow in my case,
looking through streaks of rain at the cold white sun
when all of a sudden a tram pulls up

and I could be back in Helsinki
sitting in the Café Kappeli's huge glass bay
wondering what the function of memory is,
if it has one, if that's even the right question.

Ordeal

Test us; we want to be proved, always feel
we've never been tried to the full, always
muddled through somehow, and fallen so far
short of the best that men have done. And now

there's no-one you can make that phonecall to
at 4 a.m. to break the monachal
solitude of fear or anger, as if
there's a difference; it's not fair to trouble

others. How seductive the bottle is,
the deep blue sea, coaxing the frozen knots
in the stomach. Who cares about failure? —

you can rest here, it whispers, *a long rest*
from men's eyes, and at the water's edge
you will know I am the ultimate test.

The Institution

Another day in the hive of books'
quiet babble, the girl behind the desk
gets my parcel and I untie the string
preparing to trace through sherds of lost

collections some monk's slip of the quill,
whose Latin wasn't up to scratch
nine hundred years ago, daydreaming
amidst the whirling signs and minotaurs.

Illumination unfolds today and out
of the blue God has slopped a bucket
of sunshine through leafy windows
and unlocked and dusted birdcalls

bright as a mediæval tome of songs.
I think that in the meantime
Aphrodite passed through the office
scorching a trail of naked footprints

for now the librarian, her crotch tucked
between her legs, exudes a million volts
like ultraviolet peeling skin on skin
of a palimpsest's motley polyphony.

Collage

Boots squelch, jumbo-nimble, over snails
or crunch among the native fern, the birch,
the mossy beech, the conker and the larch,
the tatty catkins of nature trails.

Just names to me — not even there
maybe — though the others found enough
to keep them swapping rough
excited whispers. Nothing to draw my stare

from something glimpsed atop a slope
of mould — a rubbish tip. Mildewed rags
somebody saved for once, rain-split sacks
of useless utensils and rotted knots of rope;

out of this coral-reef of failure
some lensless glasses catch my eye
like the empty gaze of history,
Now *that's* what I call nature.

Inscription

A hidden door in the maze, once through which
these summer days wrapped each within each
are invisible films you worm your way
inside and seal behind you like a fly
in amber; here time becomes a matrix,
a formal garden of self-enclosing walks,
its exit past the sundial etched *horam*
monstro: each Man his own Ruin makes.

Loose Change

My new house with its edges still
crisp as a minted sixpence — it could be
on one of the Greek islands, the backyard,

its whitewashed walls folding up the sun
and keeping it in its pocket.
With a new mathematics

it could be the centre of the Universe —
its just how you conceive the planets,
jiggling round an orrery in loops and rings

like the holes in a pair of jeans
clumping down the steps of a bus. Three ha'p'ny
holes in the seat of someone's jeans.

You wouldn't have thought
three discs of skin could give
such a sense of a body's intimate language,

three coins quivering at the bottom
of a wishing well. So what if beauty
is only skin deep, if it's *her* skin.

Getting on at Chingford Station

The train gags in its cat's cradle of lines.
Four down, 'the end of all aspiration',
grey minds, the end of breath, *death*, 5 letters.
I hardly notice, but for the tussle,
a schoolgirl, bland as a schoolgirl essay,

humping a cello into the carriage.
She sits with a friend, and chats wide-eyed
as if nothing had ever been said before,
as if it all still needed to be said,
dictionaries pillaged. It was like ...

someone stepped out of the door behind me
of a Tuesday morning and switched on
the sun and then went stamping across
blank sheets of snow singing hexagons
and hockets. Before he went he cocked

an ear to their fluttery voices;
all the music I never got to play
descants out of their faces — he'd snapped off
a needle of the ice and fire of youth
and slid it under my skin. It shoots.

Quartz, Quince, Sex

Everywhere the walls are invisible
as habit, remote. For the child the room
is huge plains, each with its own geography
of dust, sun and plants; only the window

shows they're walls at all. But glance through this
window's single eye, and what's outside
turns out the same as what's within, a pair
of facing mirrors' endless reflections.

Newton timed the echo in Trinity Quad,
and conned the pentagram and hexagon
for some pattern outside the wordlist. Seven
bands of colour cross the darkened room

— and viridian, mauve, magenta, cyan,
what of them? Fresh from the rowing eight and
dressed to the nines a minister declares
a decade of call it what you will.

Metamorphosis

Tattered bundles of flesh and pelt
flap in the wind at the field corner,
a coded message for the farmer,
the mole-killer's on his rounds,
stalking the ground, a gaunt
aerial, and the hair-triggered air
is taut gossamer of twitchings;
tapped into the mole's head,
he sets the traps in the long dark
ahead of himself with the tenseness
of the second before terror.
More mole than man,
mole-god, shapeshifter;
in the village he disguises this
other nature, chatting over a crust
of ale about the darts, the budget,
his sister's wedding in the autumn.

Under the Mountain

Or say that language is *not* linear,
but like a handful of stones dropped into
a stream; one, two, three, the splashes empty
and the ripples merge under the bank — some

word still lingers at the mind's fringes
even as the sentence runs on. Or say
that the experience of life is not
storiform; 'there are certain spots of time',

pockets of ore that come from different seams,
and the random links that conjure up a life.
The heat lies there just looking at you,
like a dark glaze, and closes off yesterday

and tomorrow. The path, the bridge, the stream,
the three fixed points of predestination;
in dreamlike still I walk towards the bridge.
I know I'll have to speak to them, the three

rucksacked and booted girls slumped there, aching
damply from the peak and filling the way.
Physical. I reach the crossing point
where one gets up to face me on the planks:

'Are you enough for three of us?' she said.
'Excuse me,' she said, 'is there a bus to Derwentwater?'
The air is charged with the flicker of eyes,
lightning, then darkness. 'I don't know. Sorry'

mumbled my voice; she smiled a little
and moved to let me by, her face peeping
out of its shadow. I climb on and call
my elder son whose tea is getting cold.

Word

Stepping into the bright street
everything is bigger
The warm air's
got its hands all over you
lighting the blue touch paper

The sun leafs through other days
strings them together
Yesterday in the pub
when for a few dazzling seconds
Bridget gave you her face
and it wasn't a face at all
it was her shining straight through

Has anyone noticed Bridget's black eye?
The dozy pillock
went to turn off her alarm clock
this morning
and knocked it into her face.
Shit for brains, or what!

There should be
a word for this moment
one word
tracking and backtracking
the strands and eddies
of the morning
glimmering like a chameleon
as it crosses the road
You could ramble about in it

Or you could walk out behind it
into the sun and find
a plank bench in the grass
and sitting down for a moment
see close up
the bleached and fissured wood
the insect mountaineers
swollen in a child's eye view
and be caught
by a hot flashback of joy

It would be a word
you could never finish
not in this world
not in this life
It could be
part of your name

Hidden Pond

First there is the noisy silence
of woods, crunch and crackle of step
muffled in wads of earthmould,
birdsong like the first spots
of rain, contrapuntal, scattered.
Then the tussle with bushes,
the strangled paths and no path
actually reaching the pond.
And then you're there,
or it eludes you, and all at once
a colourless patch of sky opens
the shuttering branches.
In the still you notice,
not at first, since you're not
looking for it, that the soup
of peat and twig is boiling
worse than a witches' cauldron
with mating frogs. The thing
itself. Unenmeshed
of the day to day, the memory
hints at significance, meaning.
But at the time there was only
the moment, no truth, no symbolism,
not even a mood, like an amulet,
a pebble you pick up
and keep in your pocket.

Virus

Behind the copper tiddlywinks,
the crispy fivers, the cheques
and sums and balanced statements:-

migrant swarms of volts
chirruping in microchips,
endlessly swirling, and all the while

the postmodern text of city
folds, striates. *Sighs,*
soft and starless.

What is more wonderful
than the second class ticket
and the *Daily Mail?*

The Stifled Blaze *(De onderdrukte gloed)*

The stifled blaze
of red and blue glassware
smouldering in the twilight
of a smoke-grey winter day

seen in passing
when, hardly five years old,
I was led through the Rijksmuseum
on the hand of a purposeful
grown-up.

(Hanny Michaelis, Dutch, b. 1922)

Radiographer's Mother

Here we are
Me and my friend
Walking through effects of light
And every few steps or so

I can't help but notice
She's also very dishy
Eyes have fingers
A millionth of a volt

Jumps a synapse
Like a spark
Between their digits
As God reaches out to Adam

Across the Sistine ceiling
What part of the mental swirl
Is it? Here we're chatting
About her daughter

Somewhere else
We're outside the same building
With just the slightest space
Between our hands

An infinity
Where dark worlds breed
And bend in the interphase
Of their magnetic fields

Republic

Estonian bells, the smell of brass
in winter; the world is made of words
as well as things. *More text:* a cube of stone,

the lime kiln, its siting lost in woods
of forgotten economies whose ghost
is haunting Europe; Ilsa's special

dress, all jet-black sequins, as many
as once were Tibetan monks spinning
their prayer-wheels on the roof of the world.

Dead good it was, said Hilary, gorgeous
as sin herself. In the lapping warmth
the odd thought idles across the back

of my mind; concepts, things — it was all
the same to Plato, shadows of cloudshow
in the cerebral cave; they blur and part

and merge again in new amalgams,
the lies, half-lies, credos sincerely held —
and as it happens advantageous.

Fields of Vision

1. AFRICAN MASKS, CAPETOWN, 1985

The bright clean shopping precinct like a new
till rings up its change of postcard coloured sun
on a unifying myth of bougainvillea, burger-bar
and multiple boutique. Cars and buses pile up
the hill to a University which aspires
to some reputation. Dr Schütrumpf jogs by,
the warm air tumescent, puffed up with the yeast
of Spring. People recognize each other, stop
for a coffee somewhere, coffee and chat. Outrages
happen, but most people don't see them —
or rather most people *do*, but they're black or poor
and live somewhere else, invisible behind the growls
and yelps of pain and fear.

2. CLOUDS

This time an image formed; a tropical river
deep in the interior; hot black sun above,
and edge of jungle twined in ivy.
In midriver an oarsman's racked against the current,
every muscle burning, skin peeling, his jaws
are clenched and trembling with the strain and anger
as he sees that for all the huge expense
of effort he's not going forward but slipping back
in jolts he can make up for less and less,
that from now on there is only
the current quickening and his strength
going until the boar sweeps downstream
in a remote unseen surrender.

3. STATUE OF HAVIS AMANDA, HELSINKI

So she's down at the docks showing off all her works,
apart from that, the way she looks, the way she stands,
looking along the harbourfront, cheek to the low sun,
you can tell she's a nice Finnish girl, just remembering
something she's forgotten — you could see her anyday
outside the University, in Senate Square, in Stockmann's maybe,
hesitating, coming back another day with her husband/boyfriend
to buy a slinky dress she's had her eye on, feeling a bit fat,
but he's thinking she's looking good, not thin, but not fat either.
Her sex-life, that's her business. The guide-book says the burgers
were so shocked when she first appeared they docked the sculptor's
                                                                    fee.
In pique he turned her bum to face the Government Building —
speaking for myself, I think her bum is nice.

4. SCIENCE MUSEUM (Before the Introduction of Entrance Charges)

Children run rings around the moons of Saturn.
Open-mouthed they mist the glass before
the Archimedes' screw (scale model)
that works by handle to crank a spindly
dribble from ditch to sandy field. Then
the mechanical forge where a blacksmith
grips the red hot mass beneath a hammer's
tiny blows whose wear by years accrues
to make an image of the real that's real
itself. I like the cloud-chamber, cold dark
and flecked with tracks of astral seeds —
subatomic, preverbal,
an echo takes root in the brain's dark pool.

Four Pieces for Solo Voice

1. THE GRAMMAR

Mulled wine and chestnuts. A ring
of firelit voices, and next morning's
everlasting depth of blue and gold
in frozen windows. If it's not my pain
it's yours, or someone else's
death or senility, sometime or other.

Abrupt change from indirect to direct discourse was very frequent.

2. THE GUARDIANS

Their eyes blinked in the wind,
their faces dark, wet with drops
bitterer than tears, their great
dark bottomless eyes, a job-lot
of matinee Yoricks. Funny
how the skin has holes
just where the eyes go. Says Eve,
'I could tell that Newton
a few things about apples.'

3. GULF

I like to think of Hazel
sunning herself on a Cretan beach
in a black swimsuit. Let (a)
be the net of sine-waves curving
between one moment and the next —
a nude descending a staircase, say,
beautiful as a presentation clock
received for loss of Eden. This
image obtrudes: some soldier
caught in the act of climbing
a ladder and charred rigid.
There is no 'same time as', ever.

4. MONTAGE

[Temporarily withdrawn]

Mandelbrot

I have sat days at a time, charting excursions
into the empty quarter. *Mindmap:*
a grimpen, a fen, a fog, a bog, where,
short of a thousand volts or so, thought
won't rise above the stew. Tell me a lie,

something I can believe, for the syntax
of life won't bear thinking about,
everywhere weaving its labyrinth
of infinite regressions. What can you say?

'I did it all for you.' *But it wasn't for me,*
it was for your love of me, the altar
where I was victim. They go their ways
and forget. What has truth to do with life?

Nations lie, and the story sails into myth
like the Golden Hind on a sea of words,
as fluid as the air we move in. And?

Notes:

Erwin Schrödinger (1887-1961): Austrian theoretical physicist who contributed to the theory of matter. Adopting Louis de Broglie's (1924) proposal, that particles of matter have a dual nature and in some situations act like waves, S. introduced a theory describing the behaviour of such a system by a wave equation.

Schrödinger's Cat: name give to the paradox of enquiry, that an observer's presence alters the situation to be observed. The cat is in a sound-proofed lead box. Opening or cutting the box triggers a detonator. How do you ascertain the cat's current state?

Benoit B. Mandelbrot: Franco-Polish mathematician who has been developing for the past twenty years the concept of fractals, a class of geometrical figure characterized by the radical subjectivity of their boundaries, whereby structures cannot be defined or measured in arithmetical terms because they ramify into endless and ever diminishing reproductions of themselves such that any section iterates the pattern of the whole. The concept thus resembles that of plurality without units.